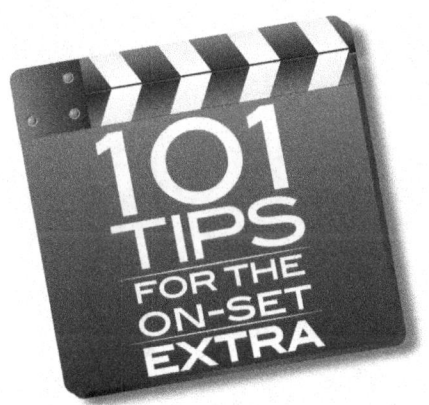

JAMIE ARINDAENG

Table of Contents

About the Author

Jamie Arindaeng is an advertising/marketing entrepreneur, owner of Visual Impact Marketing. She is also an artist and actor.

To date, Jamie has been cast several times as a featured extra, is an experienced stand-in, and has had several leading and supporting roles. Her passion for writing this book comes out of the love to help others. She is often coined "mom" on set, as she is always looking to help those who have questions or who look confused as to what is expected on set.

Jamie's other creative passion is the arts. Growing up, she often spent hours drawing or mixing together colors and textures of clothing for a fun but different style. Friends and family always commented on how creative she was at a young age. She entered several art contests in her teenage years, winning several blue ribbons. Her design and fashion acumen were a perfect fit for retail management in her earlier years. She has also worked the production side on films as the art director, prop master, and marketer.

Since she was young, Jamie had a dream of being in commercials. It was one thing to create them for her business clients, but another to actually book a local or national commercial for herself. In 2008, as the film industry was becoming more prevalent in Michigan, Jamie decided to utilize her creative and business side and learn as much as she could about the business. She spends all her free time taking acting classes, networking, and auditioning as much as possible. She is thrilled to be signed with two major Detroit talent agencies.

Jamie doesn't claim to be an expert in the film industry and she knows that all sets are not created equal. This book is simply written out of a love to help others and should be used as a guide to get you familiar with terms and protocol on most standard film sets.

Special Thanks

To my husband Geno, who always smiles when I have a new and crazy business idea: thanks for being supportive and letting me pursue my dreams.

To all my acting friends, who lent their stories from real life on set—some funny, some informative—but all with heart.

To Stacey Duford Learner, who started this crazy journey with me and has been a true friend and supporter to the end.

To you, a seasoned or new extra in the field who purchased my book. To all who will pass this along to a friend so they can learn just like you.

101 Tips for
the on-set extra

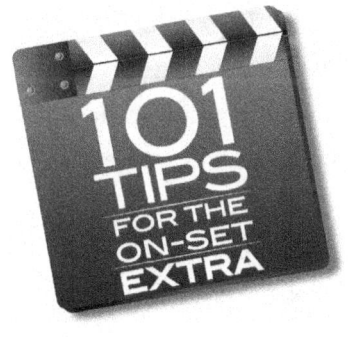

You got the job and you're going to be on-set; now what? This book is designed for the on-set working extra or background artist (as some call it). Learn everything from on set terminology and etiquette to wardrobe and make-up. Get insider secrets on how to not only survive long film shoots, but thrive and make the most of the extra opportunity.

Welcome to the exciting world of working on a movie set! It can be fun and exciting, but it's also a job, and the days are long and the cast and crew work very hard.

When you read this book you'll find that I give you information with a sense of humor, because a sense of humor will definitely be useful when you're sitting in a church basement at 3:00 a.m.

waiting to act as a funeral goer who is grieving because your favorite aunt just died. You haven't eaten since 7:00 p.m. and you're not sure when the lunch break is. Who can you find who has *any* information?

You'll find that some tips are in this book more than once. That's because they are *important* and pertain to other information in those chapters.

The bolded terms in the book are terms you will hear on-set or hear in the film industry in general. I tried to simplify most of them so they were cut- and- dry. My hope is that it will give you a better understanding of what you may hear as jargon on set. These terms are defined in the back of the book.

If you want to become an extra, check casting companies in your local area. One thing about the movie industry is that directors are seeking extras just like you. All types, sizes, shapes, and personalities need to be used in their movies. Being an extra can be great for the retired person or a mom who is an empty-nester.

I've included blank note pages in the back of the book. Use this section to take notes and/or network on set. Write down friends' phone numbers, email addresses, and Facebook™ links so when you get home you can stay connected. Go have fun on set!

Chapter One

What Does an Extra Really Do?

What can you get out of being an **extra**?

Think of it as a job, because it is. Although being on a movie **set** can be fun, it's hard work and you need to be dedicated. There are many personal reasons why you may want to do **extra** work. Maybe it's just to be in the same room with Hugh Jackman. Maybe you just want to see what it's all about and if it's for you. Maybe you're a networker and can use the time for personal growth, to meet new friends, or for business relationships. Whatever your reasons may be, keep in mind that this is a job and you need to treat it like one.

A **casting company** needs to book you and wants you to do your best. They also want you to enjoy your time on **set** and have fun. Just remember that there is a time and place for fun, but you also need to be professional. Follow the tips in this book and you should be called time and time again.

1. Your job is to make the scene look realistic. Extras don't interact with the actors in a scene (unless directed to); they are the people who happen to be in the same place as the main character.

2. Don't look at the camera.

3. Always **check in**. Sometimes you have to ask around to find the check-in person and you'll often have to wait until someone is free to check everyone in. All **sets** are not created equal.

4. Read the directions from the **casting company**. They are very thorough and spell out exactly what they expect of you.

5. Be prepared to hurry up and wait. Be patient. If you can't, then being an **extra** is not for you.

6. The pay may not be great, but this is a job. Treat it like one.

Don't be this person!
Over-Acting

Don't over-act! I remember a humorous anecdote about over-acting, when the person seemed to try to earn an Oscar as an extra. It was quite funny. The scene was set in winter, and we were supposed to be walking and window shopping. This girl was looking into the window of a store with her eyes big and a cheesy grin on her face. She made it known that she was there and I couldn't help but laugh out loud. The director finally called "cut" and asked the girl to go back to holding. It was too over the top; he was looking for natural.

Amy Slope, extra

Chapter Two

Booking
(or Getting the Job)

7. The **booking agent** or **casting company** hires or books you for the job. The **booking agent** may be someone from a private company, someone from the **production,** or even just someone with an email address who has decided he/she would like to book **extras** (and has convinced someone making a **film** that he/she can do it). This person may or may not be available on **set.** Your **paycheck** will come from the **production** company that is affiliated with the movie, not the **casting company**.

8. Read your email from the **casting company** *thoroughly!* This email will give you information for the **call time** to be on **set** and directions on how to get there.

9. If you are booked over the phone, *write down* all the information; don't rely on your memory. Directions that sound simple over the phone on a sunny

afternoon can be much more complicated at 5:00 a.m. in a strange neighborhood in the dark.

10. **Booking** has to wait until filming is finished for the day (**wrapped**) in order to get the **call time** for the next day's **extras'** work schedule. Example: if **crew** works until midnight, you may not receive your **call time** until the middle of the night. Have your smart phone handy so you can receive the email once it is sent out. Be flexible! You may be called or emailed late at night and **call times,** or **rush calls** can change or be canceled.

11. Have your **wardrobe** and **props** (if asked to bring any) ready to take to **set** with you the night before. This way all you will be waiting for is your **call time**, **location**, and where to park.

My Booking

I remember my first movie set. I was so excited. I received an email from the casting company that I was to report to set at 8:00 a.m. the next day; this was my call time. Information was attached to the email as far as a map and what type of wardrobe to bring to set. Business casual it would be. I packed some suits and off to set I went.

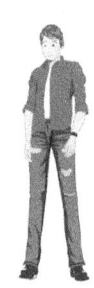

Once on set we were placed in a "holding room," where I sat with about fifty other people who all had the same dream. I waited for about an hour, while in the meantime I ate breakfast that they supplied, read a book I'd brought with me, and met some new friends. Time came to go onto the set. We all stood around a Ford car while Piper Perabo spoke at a podium. I had no idea what this set was for, as sometimes they don't tell you. I stood there for about two hours, being moved to the front, side, and back, and everywhere but where I started. They called a wrap and I went home. I was on set for five hours total. Little did I know then that it was a made-for-TV movie being shot and that a lot of times the sets are quicker and have a larger budget for things like food and water. This first experience was nothing like the next set I was on or any other after that.

Justin Allen, extra

Chapter Three

What to Bring to Work

12. Create a "**working extras kit**." This should be a small bag of things to take with you on **set** for the day. These may include a book to read, homework, etc. Whatever you may do in your down time to stay busy are some of the things you place in your bag.

13. The required **identification** (usually a driver's license and/or Social Security card or passport). Make a copy and bring it with you!

14. The required **wardrobe** and/or **props** (per your phone call or email from the **casting company**).

15. *Bring a pen!* You will be filling out a **voucher** and you may end up waiting even longer to use one of the few community pens.

16. Foods that are protein-packed and healthy and a small cooler with drinks (you'll probably need them). Sometimes the **production** will provide drinks and snacks called **craft services**, but you can't always rely on this. Again all **set**s are not created equal, nor are their budgets.

17. Something to read/do. You will spend a lot of time waiting and you may often have to be quiet. Homework, a book or crossword puzzle, a deck of cards, knitting, or even a hand-held video game system (with the audio off) will make the waiting less tedious, but keep in mind that anything you bring will remain in **holding** while you are on **set**.

18. A small, light umbrella for rain/heat. Travel pillow. Personal hand-held fan. Sanitary wipes. All these will come in handy from time to time. Trust me!

19. Phone charger—searching the Internet or playing games can really drain your battery.

20. Aspirin, antacid, gum, mints, etc. There is always a medic on **set** who will supply you with aspirin and such, but just in case you need to take a Motrin™ instead of a Tylenol™…be prepared.

21. Here's a good rule of thumb for what to bring with you: think of keeping a kid busy in church.

Anything you bring to **holding** should be small, self-contained, and quiet.

Don't be this person!
Not Prepared

I remember one set I was on. There was this annoying guy who kept asking to borrow a pen every time we had to fill out our voucher. I was nice, of course, and let him use mine—the one I'd packed and brought with me. The day went on and I noticed he was annoying in other ways as well. Not only did the pen thing bother me, but he held up the wardrobe line because he didn't bring any changes of clothes! "No way," I thought, "this guy is too much, what a clown!" As I stood there, annoyed, I thought, "This is a job; he's sure not treating it like one by following the directions and being prepared." I felt bad for his employer.

Jim Bellhop, extra

CHAPTER FOUR

WHAT NOT TO BRING TO WORK

22. Your friends, children, and/or pets. Yes, I can't believe I have to say this either.

23. A camera. You will be kicked off **set** if **production** sees you taking pictures in **holding** and/or on **set**.

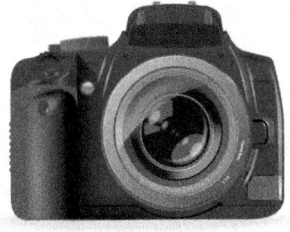

24. Photos (or anything else) for stars to sign.

25. The screenplay you wrote to show to the **director.** Yes, I'm serious. His/her time is valuable on **set** and he/she is busy making the **film**. Don't bug the **director**!

26. Valuables, cash, computers, etc. All your stuff will remain in **holding** while you are on **set**. It would be great if everyone was trustworthy, but then we wouldn't have to lock our doors now, would we?

From a PA's (Production Assistant's) Point of View

My stomach twisted a little as I looked at the large crowd staring up at me expectantly. "Ladies and gentlemen," I said, "I'm Steve, the producer. When you get off the bus, you will see a woman wearing a hat. Her name is Trish. She is your PA (boss), so do everything she tells you. Welcome to 'Deadpan'!" The group gave a cheer and bounced off the bus. I breathed a small sigh of relief. That was easy.

It was our first day of shooting with extras on our no-budget television pilot "Deadpan." Managing thirty unpaid actors was daunting, as we had no margin for error. We could not afford any reshoots and only had one chance to get this scene in the can. If any of the extras caused trouble, the entire project could collapse.

It turned out I had nothing to worry about. The group proceeded in an orderly fashion to the holding room. Everyone then patiently waited in line for make-up. They took their positions with ease and followed our directions to the letter. Their job was to laugh at our stand-up comedian's jokes, which may seem simple until you realize that they were the same jokes, take after take. Yet our "audience" laughed hard every time, as if they had never heard the jokes before. It was amazing.

There was no complaining, no egos, no drama. At the end of the long shoot, everyone was still smiling. Their enthusiasm was contagious and helped re-energize our worn-out crew. It gave all of us a huge boost and added real credibility to the project. Thanks to their professional behavior, we came away feeling, "Okay, this is really happening. We're making a show now!" We never could have done it without their support.

I know being an extra can sometimes be a thankless job, and unfortunately many producers take them for granted. For my part, I promise never to overlook their effort. An extra who is polite, positive, and patient is worth his or her weight in gold. Extras are our number-one fans and biggest supporters. That makes them family in my book.

Steve Gast, producer

Chapter Five

How Will Your Day Go: The Schedule

27. Arrive at parking. Usually a security guard will show you where to park; if not, just find the best spot in the lot.

28. Wait for **transportation** if parking is off-site from **holding**. A van or bus will shuttle you there. **Set** may or may not be where **holding** is. You may have to take **transportation** again to **set**. The **PA** will give you details once you sign in.

29. Go to **check in.** This is where you get your **voucher.** The **voucher** is how you get paid, so this is not a step to skip. If this is your second (or later) day working on the same **production**, you will write "**ON FILE**" in big letters on the back side of the **voucher.** The first-page information will still need to be filled out with your time in/out and name of the **production.** The back page can be skipped, as your information is already **on**

file for this **production**. The words **"ON FILE"** should *only* be used when you work two or more days on the same **production**.

30. See **wardrobe**. They will check to see if what you are wearing fits the **scene**, or they may supply you with clothes to wear for the day. If **wardrobe** gives you something to wear, they will take your **voucher** and hold onto it until filming is done for the day; make sure your **voucher** is filled out ahead of time, or you will have to do it late at night when you want to go home. Once you turn your clothes back in to **wardrobe,** you will get your **voucher** back and can sign out for the day.

31. Go to **holding,** where you will wait until you are called to **set**.

32. Eat **lunch,** if you work long enough (see "break" section below). Always bring some snacks and be prepared, just in case!

33. That's a **wrap**! That means the **director** has finished **shooting** for the day. You will turn in any **props** and/or **wardrobe** you used

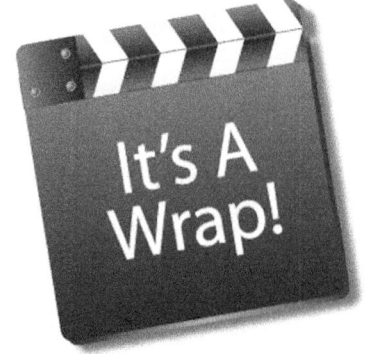

and then get your **voucher** signed. Depending on the size of the **production,** you may have to wait in line. Be patient. Everyone is tired and wants to go home. If you wait in line for half an hour you will be paid for your time. Sign out for the day.

34. **Transportation** back to parking.

Don't be this person! What a Weird but Fun Day

I was on a set for the HBO series "Hung." I remember that it was hot that day and we were filming next to the water. I was sitting inside watching the scene take place out the window. Thomas Jane was pacing back and forth and raising his hands in the air. I thought, wow, this must be an intense scene that he had with Anne Heche. That lasted about ten minutes, the scene ended, and they called for lunch. As is customary, crew eats before the extras, so I still sat. Thomas Jane entered the door and at the top of his voice said, "It's hot out there," and took his shirt off and got in line to eat. The entire room cracked up. It was nice to see an actor behave silly, as sometimes I think we place them on a different pedestal.

Justin Kline, extra

Chapter Six

DIRECTIONS/PARKING

35. **Casting** will tell you where to park and what time to be there the day prior to **set**. GPS devices are great but not always accurate, so always print out the **map** that **casting** provides. The **map** will also include a contact person in case you get lost. Allow time for parking and shuttles. You may be parking away from the **set** and need to be shuttled to the **location**.

36. When you get close to parking, there should be yellow signs on poles that read the **production** title. Example: "WHPIT" are the abbreviated initials for a **set** called "Whip It." The **production** letters will be bolded with an arrow. Follow these signs to parking.

37. Once you get to the parking area, *park there*. Do not look for parking on the street, another lot, etc. Your car may be towed or you may have to pay for parking. Any costs you incur from parking in the wrong place are not reimbursed by **casting**.

Look for the Signs

I'd received the email from casting with the address for the set the night before, so I was ready to go, or so I thought. I used my GPS to guide me there, but little did I know it wouldn't be 100% accurate. My GPS said I was there, yet the building looked abandoned to me. "Great. Now what?" I called the person listed to call in case of emergency on the map I printed out, but there was no answer. I left a voice mail. I was going to be late and was getting stressed. I started to look around and saw a yellow sign on a pole nearby with the letters "HALF" and an arrow on it. It dawned on me. "HALF"—Have a Little Faith—that's the set! I followed the arrow and saw a parking lot full of cars. "This must be it!" I asked the parking attendant, who confirmed I was in the correct spot. Next time I will always look for the signs.

Jason Bernick, extra

Chapter Seven

I Said I Was Available to Work; Why Wasn't I Called?

38. There are many reasons you may not have been called. First, **casting** may have filled the **scene** before they got to your "yes" reply. They may also have been looking for more people of the opposite gender, or may simply have too many people of your ethnicity already in the **background**. Don't take it personally.

My Hurt Ego

My friends got the email saying they were chosen for set the following day, yet I wasn't. "What went wrong?" I thought. "I'm cute, I said I was available; why wasn't I chosen?" My ego took a beating that day. I later learned that they had too many girls for the scene and needed more guys. It wasn't about me after all. I learned a lesson that day. "Ego," I said, "it's not always about you!"

Susanne Ghram, extra

Chapter Eight

On Set

Location is the place you are **filming**. Yes, it's called that. Some things are just as simple as they sound.

39. The **call time** is the time you are expected to arrive on **set**. As a rule of thumb, always be a little early. Most **production**s prefer you to be fifteen minutes early.

40. Depending upon the size of the **production,** there may be a long line to **check in.** Yes, you can play Angry Birds™ on your phone while you are in line, but be ready to go when you finally get to the front or you may find yourself surrounded by angry co-workers.

41. The person (**PA**) who checks you in is probably doing ten other jobs as well. *And* this person is usually the first person who decides who gets on **set** and where you will be placed. Behave professionally, as you should at any job.

42. The **PA** or **AD (Assistant Director)** will place you and give you a **direction**. Don't be a camera hog! The harder you try, the less likely it is that you will be placed in an ideal spot. Don't beg to be in front of the camera. You will see the same **PAs** on different **sets**…they do remember the annoying people! Once you are in place, there may be a few **rehearsal**s. You will get feedback from the **PA** if you're not doing what the **director** wants you to do, or if he/she would like you to do something different.

43. When **background** is called by the **PA** you need to move (act) as if you're really in that **scene**. Example: if you're at the mall, look like you're shopping, talking (**pantomiming**, see below) with a friend, talking on a cell phone, etc. Do what you would normally do in that setting. You may hear terms like **pictures up, rolling, cut, back to one,** and **background. Background** is your cue to move.

44. Do the same movement (**direction**) for every take…this is called **continuity.**

DON'T BE THIS PERSON!
BEHIND THE SCENE

One of my experiences on set is one that every extra or even PA should be aware of what not to do. There was an extra on set one day who was curious about the production and what goes on behind the scenes. It's awesome to have someone interested and wanting to learn how things run, but the issue was that he kept trying to talk with the director. He kept trying to ask the director questions about the screenplay he was writing during filming and it was hard for the director to get his job done. As a result,

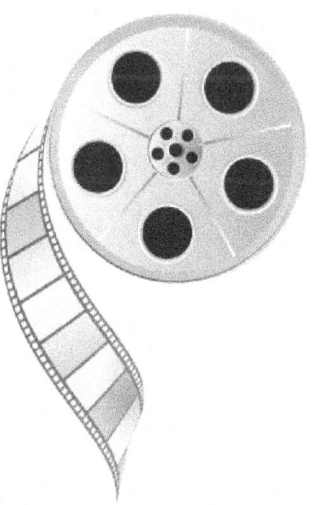

one of the other crew members and I had to make sure to keep him away from the director. That was an unnecessary task we did not need to add to our already busy job. Whether you know the director or not, you need to know the boundaries when you are on a set. Unfortunately, he was not asked to come back to set again.

Ashley Gray, extra

Chapter Nine

Fame

45. It is unlikely that anyone will be watching a movie and suddenly say, "See that guy in the crowd scene with the red shirt? I *must* have him as the lead in my next movie!" An **extra** is there to make the **scene** look more realistic. If someone sees a movie you worked on but didn't see you, that's the biggest compliment you can get. You did your job well and stayed out of the way. If you want to be famous someday, take some acting lessons and get a job waiting tables to help pay the bills in the meantime. If you want to learn about the business, keep busy working, network by meeting lots of people, and have fun working a lot as an **extra**. With training come opportunities.

My Day of Fame

The night before, I got the call from casting. They told me they wanted to switch me. I was booked on another set, and suddenly I had the opportunity to audition for the role of Mrs. Jillian

Moscone in the movie "Trust." The next day, after speeding down dirt roads and circling the enormous depths of the Dexter High School parking lot to find the only open spot, I arrived. Already terribly late, I hurried to grab my bags of wardrobe changes and hair and make-up supplies, then promptly locked my purse, keys, phone, lip balm, and gum in my car. I held my shopping bags of borrowed clothing close to my chest, took a deep breath, then ran (in heels), not breathing, searching for the right door to the extras' holding.

Two mini-doughnuts and several uncomfortable introductions later, David Schwimmer came in to choose between one other hopeful and me. By default, I got the part. Blonde-haired, blue-eyed daughter (Cassi Fitch), blond-haired, blue-eyed husband (Joey Sikora), BINGO! Casting is like a birth-giving process. We actually looked related. Sometimes it's about what you look like, and not what you can do. As luck would have it I got my own trailer, breakfast and all. Dreams do come true.

Erica Blair, upgraded extra

Chapter Ten

Holding and Waiting in Lines: the "Rules" of Holding

46. **Holding** is where you will spend the majority of your time. How comfortable it is depends on the size of the **extra cast** and where you are **shooting**. You could be waiting in a basement, a gymnasium, a tent outdoors (in the heat or cold), a hotel lobby, or any number of places.

The "Rules" of Holding

47. Be respectful.

48. Always clean up after yourself.

49. Don't take up more space than you need, especially if it's crowded.

50. Never leave a **set**!

Don't be this person!
Space Hog

One girl in holding took up three chairs. I walked in, looking for a seat in the crowded room. There was nothing. I politely asked the girl if I could have one of her chairs and she declined, saying, "This is all my stuff." It's one thing to be prepared for set; it's another to bring your house and take up the room. I finally got a seat, as a PA had to ask her to place her stuff on the floor next to her.

Justin Reamer, extra

Chapter Eleven

Things You Will Wait in Line For

51. To sign in.

52. To sign out.

53. To get **wardrobe** approved.

54. To eat **lunch**.

55. For the **props** department to give you **props** or to return **props** (if necessary).

All Sets Are Not Created Equal

I remember my first movie set—"Whip It," directed by Drew Barrymore. Our call time was 5:00 a.m. in Detroit. I brought a few things for wardrobe like the casting company had asked us to do; I was ready and excited to work. I pulled up at an old abandoned steel mill and thought, "This is going be a cool set!" I signed in, went through wardrobe and had a seat. I saw a table of breakfast items and people eating, so I also had something. The day went on filming, with us in the stands as crowd goers. It was over 100 degrees in the building. No lie! The PAs tried to cool us down with a fan with a splash of water attached to a hose, but that didn't work, as the crowd was large. I was getting hungry and tired. Six hours passed and it was lunch time, finally! I was starving. We rushed through the line to grab food. It was running low before everyone got to eat—thank God I was toward the front of the line. We got about a twenty-minute break, then off to set again, back in the hot stands to scream like fans. The day went on and it was 8:00 p.m., 11:00 p.m. "What the heck?" I thought. I asked a PA when we were going to get some food or a break; the answer was "soon." The day ended the following morning at 6:00 a.m.—it had been a twelve-hour day! I had not been prepared for that. I was tired and hungry. I learned that not all sets are created equal. Drew was new to directing. She was passionate about her film and she wanted it done right. I just wished I had been that passionate about thinking ahead and taking some snacks with me to set.

Marcus Jones, extra

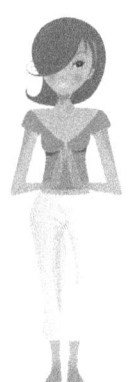

56. **Here's a health tip for standing in line to help relieve pressure on your back:** stand in yoga Mountain Pose. You will be conscious of your standing position, including your feet, legs, hips, and back. This pose will improve circulation, reduce fatigue, and create a state of mindfulness, a way to help yourself while others are just standing around waiting.

To do Mountain Pose:

Stand in position - Stand tall and upright with your feet hip-width apart and parallel to one another. Distribute your weight evenly between your feet and on the three weight-bearing parts of each foot: the heel, the ball of the foot at the base of the big toe, and the ball of the foot at the base of the little toe.

Side note: a variation on this pose calls for a narrower base by positioning your legs and feet together, their inner edges touching.

Align hips

Your hips should be aligned directly over your legs, which should be aligned directly over your feet.

Side note: keep in mind the idea of balance throughout this pose. Balance is an integral part of yoga, both physically and spiritually.

Lengthen lower back

Allow your tailbone to drop, lengthening your lower back. To help yourself do this, imagine a fishing weight attached to your tailbone, steadily pulling it down. The weight of your upper body should be transferring through your pelvis into the hip joints in such a way that you can feel your pelvis balancing on the tops of your femur bones.

Center shoulders

Center your shoulders between the front and back of your body, in a neutral position. When you find the right spot, the upper back should feel relaxed and free of any unwanted tension.

Align shoulders and back

With your shoulders and upper back properly aligned, your head should feel like a helium-filled balloon on a string floating up off your neck.

Hold pose

Breathe normally, and hold this pose for as many breaths as you like.

Side note: because the Mountain Pose is so simple, it can be practiced anywhere at anytime—in line at the grocery store, during a ride in the subway, or even at a concert with friends.

Release pose

To release the pose, simply relax. And you thought you knew how to stand.

Chapter Twelve

Wardrobe

57. The basic **wardrobe** consists of simple, conservative separates in plain neutral colors. You'll need clothing for all seasons (your **scene** could take place in Michigan in the winter, yet you're to be in a **scene** that takes place in Arizona in the summer).

58. Often you'll be asked to bring two or more options of clothing with you. You might think it's unimportant, but if everyone shows up wearing black, the scene will not look realistic. Bring options!

Don't be this person!
Didn't Think about the Shoes

I was gathering my dress for the wedding rehearsal set the next morning. I stuck some tennis shoes in my bag, thinking no one would see my shoes because I would be wearing a long gown…just like some brides do on their wedding day. I got to set, signed in, and went through wardrobe. They asked to see my dress options and shoe options. "Shoe options," I thought—oops! I showed them my tennis shoes and explained that my feet wouldn't be seen. To my surprise, there was a scene where they wanted the wedding party to do the can-can and kick up their legs in a line as a joke to the bride. Luckily wardrobe had an extra pair of shoes for me to borrow.

Wendy Mack, extra

Clothing

59. Don't bring clothing with large/obvious logos and/or labels. You're not paid to be a walking billboard.

60. Avoid loud prints.

61. Don't wear white. It doesn't work well on camera.

62. The **wardrobe** department will look at your clothing options and tell you what to wear on **set**. That's right; it's not up to you.

DON'T BE THIS PERSON! WRONG STYLE, LADY

Yes, your style is important, but basic neutral clothes are what wardrobe directors are looking for. I once saw a woman not get to work on set because she showed up as a "Lady Who Lunches" with only artsy/grunge-style clothes. She obviously would have stood out, so they chose to leave her

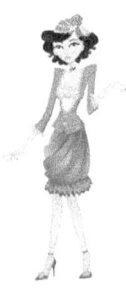

out instead. She sat on set all day and was not used. I wondered why she didn't bring the variety of clothing options that the email from casting suggested. If you don't fit into the category casting is looking for—and yes, that means wardrobe as well—opt out. Not every set is for everyone, just as not every profession is for everyone. This is a job and should be treated as one.

Densie Kelp, extra

Chapter Thirteen

Hair and Makeup

63. Your **hair** should coordinate with your role. Showing up as a mall shopper with a fancy up-do will probably get you sitting in **holding** all day and not working.

64. Simple and understated **make-up** is best.

65. You should be given some kind of **direction** from **casting** for **hair** and **make-up**. If not, go with a normal, everyday look. It's easier to amp you up than to bring your look down.

Don't be this person!
Blue Eye Shadow

I couldn't stop staring at the older lady on set. Her eyelids were caked with heavy blue eye shadow. I remember that in the 80s I wore this style, but today it was so out of style. I chuckled inside. To make it even funnier, the scene was for a period piece,

1920s-style movie. They didn't wear make-up like that back then. What was she thinking, and why didn't she come in the natural make-up detailed in the email from casting?

Sandy Rainer, extra

Chapter Fourteen

Breaks and Lunch

66. Most **productions** are part of the **union. Union films** have to abide by **union** laws. They take mandatory **breaks** for **lunch** after working a certain number of hours. A good rule of thumb is that **lunch break** occurs six hours after **crew call time** (which may or may not be the same as *your* **call time**). Example: if **crew call time** is 9:00 a.m., **lunch break** would be around 3:00 p.m., and you may work until 9:00 p.m. at night without another **lunch break**.

67. Many departments on **set** belong to different **unions (guilds)**. Example: art directors, lighting, **actors,** and sound all belong to different **unions**.

68. Being an **extra** doesn't always mean you will eat **lunch** on **set**. Your **call time** may begin after the **lunch break**. Be prepared and always eat before you get to **set**! You may not arrive on **set** until 4:00 p.m. and **crew** has already eaten.

I Was Starving

My call time was 11:00 a.m. for set. I didn't have time to eat, as I'd received a rush call that morning. "No worries," I thought, "I can get lunch on set." Time went by—six hours and no lunch. "Hmm, that's weird," I thought. I asked a PA when lunch would be served and she said they'd already eaten. The crew call time was 4:00 a.m. that morning; they had lunch at 10:00 a.m. Oh no, now what? Sure, there was a craft services food table, but that was just chips and water. That wouldn't really sustain me. Thank God I'd packed some snacks for just-in-case purposes! I ate my pre-packed tuna and crackers with my apple and went on working with energy and a smile.

Rick Waters, extra

69. If you have special dietary requirements (i.e. vegan or food allergies) there may be options for you, but don't count on it. Going through the food line is usually fast and there is often no one to ask about what *exactly* is in the sauce. Bring your own food if you have real concerns.

Get Prepared the Night Before

Grabbing a bag of chips and candy can be the easiest thing to do when you're not prepared, but taking time the night before to pack a good, healthful snack will leave you energized and not regretting the food you ate while on set. I like to pack the pre-packed tuna that comes with crackers and some fruit. I also bring some nuts and water. Protein is key when you can't eat for a long period of 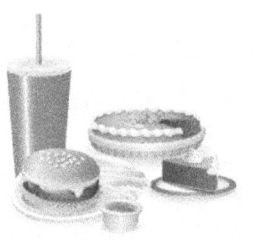 *time. I was on a set once that was a fourteen-hour day. We ate lunch after six hours, then received nothing the rest of the night. The girl next to me was diabetic and had no food with her (as this was her first set). Thank God I had a piece of fruit left, which I shared with her.*

Judy Sunguard, extra

Chapter Fifteen

Who's Who on the Set

70. The **stand-in** or **second team** is the person who stands in for an **actor**. (This person does not need to be a body double, but does need to look similar to the **actor** and be generally the same height.) The **stand-in** will be asked to perform the actions of the **actor** so the **crew** can get camera and lighting ready before the **actor** comes on to **film**. The **stand-in** generally makes a higher hourly pay than an **extra**.

71. As a **stand-in**, you are responsible for watching the **scene** so you know where to stand, what to do, etc. You will be asked by **casting** to match color cover...this means if the **actor** is wearing navy blue pants and a green shirt, the **stand-in** should wear the same.

72. The **PA – production assistant** (Your boss!) This is the person(s) who will sign you in/out and who will guide you on **set**. The **PA** will be in **holding** with you. Did we mention that the **PA** is your boss? Listen to the **PA** for your **directions** and try to stay quiet while the **PA** is talking. Most of the time, the **PA** will not have a megaphone and may have to scream over a large crowd. Sit toward the front of the room so you can hear and be prepared for **set**.

73. **AD – assistant director**

74. The **director** – the big boss

75. **DOP – director of photography**

76. **Prop master** – Person who handles the **props** for each **scene** on **set**. Don't ask this person or others on **set** if you can use the bathroom…they do **props**! Find the **PA** (your boss!)

77. If you are given a **prop**, you must return it to the **prop master** at the end of the **scene** or end of the day, unless you are told otherwise.

WHO'S WHO?

Understanding everybody's role will help you get a leg up as a working extra…take the time to learn a little about every type of job on set, if for nothing else than to help you stay out of the way!

Jim Canning, producer

CHAPTER SIXTEEN

WHAT IS A FEATURED EXTRA?

78. A **featured extra** is just that. You're featured, or seen on camera. It doesn't necessarily mean that when the movie or show comes out you will be seen; the editing process takes time and things get cut. What it does mean is that once you are featured, you probably won't work much the rest of the day on other **scenes**. The **director** needs to see new faces on **film**. If you were already seen, you were seen. It also doesn't mean that you're special and get more pay or that you can now eat with the **cast** and **crew**.

I WAS FEATURED

I was asked to be a featured extra once I got to set. What did that mean, I thought? I was excited yet kind of nervous. Would I speak? I was placed in front of the crowd rather than in the far background. This is what featured meant: close up. The director liked my look and gave me and a few other extras microphones to act as reporters. It was exciting! The TV series finally aired and I was so excited to see if my scene made the final cut. It did, and there I was with a group of other featured extras playing reporters. It was cool. I received the same pay as an extra that day, but was so proud to be seen on TV.

Allen Marks, featured extra

Chapter Seventeen

Congratulations! You've Been Upgraded!

79. A **director** may choose to give an **extra** a line to say or ask you to work as a **stand-in** for a scene, or ask to use your car. This changes your category and, most importantly, what you get paid. The pay is different for each **upgrade**. If you are **upgraded**, tell the **PA** in charge (in case the **PA** doesn't hear the **director**) and DO NOT leave the **set** until you get your proper paperwork filled out with your **upgrade** included. If you were given a line, you will receive **SAG** paperwork. If you were asked to use your car, the **PA** will need to change that status on your **voucher** so you receive the extra pay. It's usually $25.00, on top of your hourly rate, if **production** chooses to use your car in a **scene**.

My Upgrade

You know that guy in the movie everyone talks about, he is referenced here and there, but you never really get a chance to see him? That was me in a movie called "Lunatics – A Love Story," executive produced by the one and only Sam Raimi. Yes, the movie was a flop by Hollywood standards, but it did wonders for me. It earned me my SAG card through Taft-Hartley and I am forever grateful. I played the lead's (Ted Raimi's) brother, and although I was an extra in the movie (and if you blink you'll miss me), I had a great time on the set. I was given the royal treatment and shared a trailer with Ted and a few others. I was living my dream, and honestly, if I had died the next day I would've died a happy man, having just been in a movie.

You never know who you'll meet or what can happen on set. The producer might see you, like your look, and move you up to a speaking roll. Being an extra can open up many doors. Take advantage of every chance you get. I still kick myself for turning down an opportunity to work on the movie "61." I thought I was too good to be an extra then, but given the chance today I would jump at it, if for no other reason than to make contacts and friends.

Tim Courtney, upgraded extra to SAG

I Showed Up, Got Wardrobe, Waited in Holding, Ate Lunch, but Never Worked on Set—What Happened?

80. **Production** may have started placing **extras** in a **scene** and realized they had too many before you got called to **set**. A **film** or TV **set** is frequently a fluctuating environment and plans change. The key to working as an **extra** is flexibility. If you didn't get to work on **set** that day, you still get paid.

You Might Not Want This to Happen to You

A kid on a set was super-excited to be given a line and to be upgraded in pay. However, this was on the first day of shooting and he was scheduled to work ten days. Once you are paid an actor's rate for one day, you must be paid that rate for any other day(s) you work (instead of at the extra rate), so he was sent home at the end of that day because of budget (they couldn't afford to keep using him.) My point here is to take it slow. Don't be overly zealous in wanting to be upgraded. Sure, it has its perks, but as you just read, it can also leave you not working on set the rest of the remaining days scheduled. Editing is a long process where lots of cuts can happen (it's called the cutting room floor). I've been on the cutting room floor lots of times, so don't take it personally. Perhaps even more frustrating than not getting a chance to perform, is the feeling of having wasted your time. Be sure to find another way to be productive while on set, so that at the end of the day you can go home with a sense of accomplishment, even if you didn't get to work on the rest of the set.

Christina Howard, extra

Chapter Nineteen

How to Get Kicked Off the Set—Yes, it Can Happen!

81. Taking photos, or posting them on websites, Twitter™, Facebook™, MySpace™, etc. Talking with the media. Sure, it's exciting and you want the world to know that you're going to be in a movie, but imagine if media and friends find out and all show up to **set**. What a distraction!

82. Not following **directions**.

83. Talking on **set**. Unnecessary talking makes it hard to understand what you are supposed to do. Never talk while someone in charge is talking; it is so annoying and just downright rude. Often people ask each other what the **PA** said while the **PA** is speaking, and it is difficult to hear new information because of it.

84. Leaving **set**. Stay put; this is your job for the day.

Don't be this person! Smile and Say Cheese

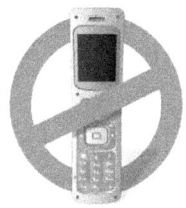

From the production's perspective, privacy about a film is important. They are the ones creating the images and the art, so it's theirs to do with what they please, not yours. Everyone is an amateur photographer these days with their camera phone, but people are getting a paycheck to make the film only because the production made those pictures possible; they're not for your camera. Bottom line: leave your cameras at home and your cell phone in holding.

Raymond Hiller, producer

My Child Is the Extra: What Do I Do?

85. All of the rules and schedules apply to you as well as to your child. The only difference is that when your child is taken to **set,** most of the time you will remain in **holding**. Don't try to sneak on **set** and watch your child. Don't be a stage mom or dad! If you were told to stay in **holding**, stay there.

86. If your child is allergic to peanuts or anything else, tell the **PA** right away. The **craft foods** table usually has these items on it and people will be eating them in **holding**.

87. Don't bring other children to work with you who are not working on the **production**.

88. Don't pester the **PA** with questions about when your child will work.

89. Bring books, games, homework, to keep your child occupied and quiet.

My Kid's Working, Yea!

The day I got to set with my kid I wasn't sure what to expect, as this was his first time filming. I saw a group of parents sitting together and eventually joined them after signing in; they seemed very friendly. I began to hear how "little Dave" was a star, from his mom Christine. She said he had been in over twenty films so far, how he was a featured extra, and so on. She seemed to know it all about the industry, yet Dave seemed unfazed. I sat there thinking, "So what?" Another stage mom wanting her child to make it; I get that. I didn't get her behavior throughout the day as she kept pestering the PA, asking when Dave was going to be on set, when would they eat, when, when? "Enough," I thought and excused myself and moved with my child to another section in the holding room.

Sheeree Ramirez, extra

CHAPTER TWENTY

TALKING/PANTOMIME

90. As an **extra** you will never talk during a **scene**. You will **pantomime**. This means fake talking by moving your lips with no sound coming out. This does not mean whispering. If 200 **extras** whisper, it sounds like a very loud tire leak. Quiet is key. Keep facial expressions natural, smile, nod your head, expressing that you are having a real conversation on screen, even though you are not.

HOW TO TALK WITHOUT TALKING

Here's how I portray pantomiming on set:

- *I repeat the alphabet slowly over and over: a, b. c, d....*

- *I pantomime nonsensical gibberish with facial expressions to match the scene. I have used the words 'cheese and crackers' and 'watermelon' a lot.*

- *One time on set I talked with a girl who was my scene partner and we were flirting back and forth by pantomiming things like, "What's your number? Do you come here often?" That was fun and made us both laugh so it really looked like we were having a real conversation.*

Dennis Budzizewski, extra

Chapter Twenty-one

Props

91. You may be asked to use your own **prop**s on **set**—a purse, bag, notebook—anything you bring with you that may fit into the 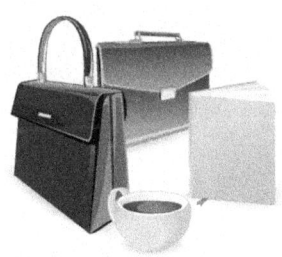 scene. The **prop master** will look at your stuff and give you approval as to what to use.

92. If you are given a **prop** from the **prop**s department, you are responsible for that **prop** until it is given back to the **prop**s department. Do not change it in any way, lose it, or take it home. The bulky heavy cell phone from the 90s may be cool, but if it ends up 'missing,' so is your pay for the day.

My Prop

On the set of "Naked Angel" I was given a notepad as my prop. The scene was set in the park and I was a featured extra who was supposed to be thinking and drawing my thoughts. The camera was above me to show the notepad and my drawing. Thank God I could draw, but that had already been decided when the director asked who on set could draw, and I raised my hand. The scene took several takes, using up most of the notepad. At the end of filming I had to return my prop in order to receive my voucher back so I could get paid.

Jeff Wilson, extra

CHAPTER TWENTY-TWO

I WANT TO BE A SAG/AFTRA ACTOR!! HOW TO JOIN SAG/AFTRA

93. SAG (**Screen Actors Guild**) is a **union** for **actors**. Rules and fees for joining vary from state to state. Check the **SAG** website or call your local **SAG** office to check the rules and requirements on how to join the **union** in your state.

94. AFTRA (**American Federation of Television and Radio Artists**): any person who has performed or intends to perform professional work in any one of AFTRA's jurisdictions is eligible for membership. Contact your local office for specific information about **AFTRA** membership and its benefits.

Note: As of 2012 **SAG** and **AFTRA** have merged. The new name is SAG-AFTRA Union

http://www.sag-aftra.org

Chapter Twenty-three

Other Important Stuff

95. **Head shots** – These should be current. If you have changed your hair color and/or style, grown or shaved off facial hair, then update your photos with **casting**. Don't spend a ton of money on these— ask your friends whom they used or know who can take a headshot that shows your face close up.

96. Remember that you are being booked based on what you look like, and if you show up looking different you may be sent home.

97. Your **resume** (yes, spelling counts) – Keep your **resume** updated, and use spellchecker and/or a proofreader. You should never list your **extra** work on your acting **resume** under the **film** section. Rather, include a statement that might say "experienced **extra**" under the skills section toward the bottom. Depending on what type of audition you attend, you should list those experiences that relate most significantly to that job at the top of your

resume. Example: if you are auditioning for a **film** role, list your **film** credits-shorts, or featured- at the top, follow with theater experience, and so on. **Directors** want to see the experience you have had on **set** and in front of the camera. Being an **extra** won't always give you the skills you need to be comfortable close up in front of the camera. Look for acting opportunities at local colleges, **film** schools, and on the Internet. Stay active in acting and doing theater; these opportunities will make you more comfortable in front of the camera and ready when you do get that part.

98. **Acting Schools** – There are several great acting schools throughout the country that can help you take your craft to the next level. Do a search online or ask your friends what classes they are taking or have taken. If you want to become more than just an **extra**, you will need training. Look into theater classes as well. Theater is different from **film**, but these classes can give you some valuable tips on how to hone the craft of acting in general. Working in front of a live audience is very different from working on **film**. It would benefit you as an **actor** to learn each craft.

99. **Talent Agents** – Check your local area for reputable talent **agents**. Once you have training and a

good **head shot**, you should talk with an **agent** and sign up to be in the **agent's** talent pool. The **agent** you sign with should be free. The same thing applies to **casting** companies in your area. These agencies make a percentage off jobs they book for you, so paying to have an **agent** is paying them twice! If a **casting company** asks for a small fee, never pay more than $25.00. Also, watch out for scammers who say they can get your kid on Disney™ by paying them $2,500 and they will do all the work for you. Don't believe it! You are your hardest worker, **agent** or not. Find the work through networking and talking with your acting friends. There are several reputable websites for acting jobs. Here are two: www.mandy.com and www.actorsaccess.com.

100. **Networking** – Meeting new people can be new and exciting, but how will your new friend remember you and stay in touch? Sure, you can find some scrap paper to write your information on, but better yet, hand out a calling card. So many online printers offer business cards at a discounted price. Make a card for yourself to pass out on set. Make sure to include your photo along with your email address and phone number so your new friend remembers you. Be sure to order enough to hand out to anyone you encounter along your talent journey.

*Also check the back page of this book for blank notes page.

101. **IMDB (International Movie Data Base)** has become very popular with **extras** over the last few years. The website was created for acting professionals to list their credentials in TV, **film**, and such. Membership can easily be obtained through **IMDB**, and you can list your experience on the site. However, it should *not* be used for any **extra** work that you have done. Too many **extras** I know are listing their work as a **background** artist and it can cause issues with the **production** company. You were not **cast** in the **film** by the **director** and are not making the big bucks (yet), so leave your information off the site. The **producer** in charge of each **production** will include your information on **IMDB** if applicable.

IMDB ISSUES

This is a message from a **casting company** to all the extras who worked on this production:

I received a call from HHFP (Hallmark Hall of Fame Productions) a couple of hours ago. If you were an extra on "Have a Little Faith" and gave yourself a credit on IMDB, please delete it. The listings have been creating problems between HHFP and SAG.

Ryan Hill, Ryan Hill Casting

For more information on **IMDB** visit: http://www.imdb.com and http://en.wikipedia.org/wiki/internet_movie_database.

That's a Wrap!

I hope this book was useful on your journey as an extra. I sincerely hope you follow these tips with common sense and judgment, as I have stated not all sets are created equal.

This book should be used as a fun, quick roadmap to help guide you along your acting journey. Good luck wherever you end up. **Break a leg**!

Have a comment or question?
Visit us at 101tipsfortheonsetextra.wordpress.com
and on Facebook.

Chapter Twenty-Four

TERMS

Acting School – a place one goes to study the art of acting.

Actor or actress – a person who acts in a dramatic production and who works in film, television, theatre, or radio in that capacity.

AFTRA – the American Federation of Television and Radio Artists is a performers' union that represents a wide variety of talent, including actors in radio and tele-vision, as well as radio and television announcers and newspersons, singers and recording artists (both royalty artists and background singers), promo and voice-over announcers and other performers in commercials, stunt persons, and specialty acts.

Agent – person or company who represent you as an actor. An agent finds work for you and has you come in to audition for clients. An agent receives a percentage of your actual bookings.

Assistant Director (AD) – assistant director of the film. In theater, the AD is called the artistic director.

Background – Means you (the extra) and is your cue to "act" your scene, use your prop, pantomime, etc.

Back to one – Your cue to begin your scene over and go back to where you first started.

Booking (same as casting company) – employment for actors that lasts for a limited period of time.

Breaks – If you're sitting in holding and not on set, that is your break. Union laws require a lunch break six hours after the crew call time. If crew came in at 6:00 a.m. and your call time is 1:00 p.m., you missed lunch. Be prepared with your own food just in case. (See lunch)

Break a leg – a well-known idiom in theatre that means "good luck." It is typically said to actors and musicians before they go on stage to perform. The origin of the phrase is obscure. To "break the leg" or "break a leg" is archaic slang for bowing or curtsying; placing one foot behind the other and bending at the knee "breaks" the line of the leg. In theatre, pleased audiences may applaud for an extended time, allowing the cast to take multiple curtain calls, bowing to the audience.

Bump or Upgrade – you're a reporter in a scene (non-speaking featured extra). The director may ask you to say a line or two. Great! This is called a bump and you will receive a pay increase (check the SAG laws in your state for the amount). You may also be asked to use your car in a scene; again this is a bump in pay. Your voucher will be marked at the end of the day. Make sure to never leave set until this is done. It's almost impossible to dispute once you leave for the day.

Call Time – your time to be at holding. If your call time is 6:00 a.m. and you live an hour away, make sure you account for traffic, etc., and getting lost. Always arrive fifteen minutes prior to your call time just to be safe. (see map)

Cast – all actors who are working on the set for the day.

Casting Company – the company from whom you get the job.

Check In – the place or location you will check in for the day. You will get your voucher at this point. Sit down and fill it out.

Cinematographer – person photographing with a motion picture camera (the art and science of which is known as cinematography). The title is generally equivalent to Director of Photography (DOP).

Craft Services – the people responsible for supplying snacks, water, etc. in the holding room for extras. This does not always happen, as some budgets are small. Be prepared and bring a few snacks of your own.

Crew – the persons working on the set for the film. These include the PA, AD, prop master and others.

Continuity – doing the same thing in a scene. Example: you walked into the room with a friend, you were on the right. When you're asked to do it again, and again, you will do the same thing. Walk into the room with your friend on the person's right side. Remember what you did and where you were….it's important to the scene.

Cut – to stop the scene. The director may call cut for several reasons. There may be an issue with the camera, the scene may have started late, or an actor may have forgotten the lines.

Cutting Room Floor – once the editing process is done, your scene may not make the cut due to length of the film or several other reasons beyond your control.

Director – the big boss, the person in charge of the film.

Director of Photography (DOP) or **Cinematographer** – the person responsible for making scenery look good and the actors look even better.

Direction – a cue given to you by the PA as what they want you to do in the scene: where to walk, turn a corner, etc.

Extra/ Extra Cast – an actor who fills in the background of a scene. Also called background artist.

Featured Extra – an extra who is prominently seen on camera; i.e. a reporter or vendor, etc. This does not mean you will be seen or that you will speak (although sometimes a director may ask you to). (see bump)

Film – the movie you are working on.

Guilds – a guild (German: gilde) is an association of craftsmen in a particular trade. Groups actors join include SAG, AFTRA, and many more.

Hair – your hairstyle for the day. If you're on a 1950s film, hair stylists will be on set to make your hair look like that era. Otherwise, be natural-looking and don't pile on the hairspray and tease it like crazy (unless you're told to come to set that way).

Head Shot – a professional photo that can be given to casting companies. A good head shot doesn't need to be expensive, but should be a good up-close shot to showcase your facial features.

Holding – a room or location where all extras wait to work on set. This is your spot for the day, where you will stay put until you are called to set.

Identification – a passport or driver's license is required at check in.

Location – the place where the movie is being filmed.

Lunch – union laws require a lunch break six hours after the crew call time for that day's work. So if crew came in at 6:00 a.m. and your call time is 1:00 p.m., you missed lunch. Again, be prepared with your own food just in case.

Make-Up – same as hair (see above). Keep it simple!

Map – the casting company will supply you with an emailed map of the parking location for your day on set. The map will include a phone number to call in case you get lost.

On File – this means you have worked on this same set more than once. If that is the case, you will write ON FILE on your voucher under the I-9 section. The I-9 does not need to be filled out again as your info is on file already.

Pantomime – the art or technique of conveying emotions, actions, feelings, etc. by gestures without speech. This means moving your lips as if you are speaking, but no sound is coming out…not even a whisper!

Paycheck – you will receive payment for work done on the set in the form of a check through the mail. This information comes from filling out your voucher…make sure it's readable and all information is correct! You will usually receive your check about two weeks from the date of work. Your paycheck does not come from the casting company, but rather from the production company in charge of the film. There is a phone number on the voucher form that you will keep for your records. Use this number if you encounter any problems receiving your pay after a few weeks.

Pictures up – a term you will hear on set called from the director. This simply means the director is letting his crew know that he is almost ready to roll the film footage and start.

Producer – person who initiates, coordinates, super-vises, and controls matters such as fund-raising, hiring key personnel, and arranging for distributors for a film. The producer is involved throughout all phases of the film-making process, from development to completion of a project.

Production – the movie/TV show/commercial itself… the whole process

Production Assistant (PA) – a job title used in film-making and television for the person responsible for various aspects of a production. The PA's job can vary greatly, depending on the budget and specific require-ments of a production, as well as whether or not the production is unionized.

Prop – an object to be handled by the actors or extras in a scene, such as a newspaper or coffee cup.

Prop Master – the person(s) responsible on set for having the props for the scenes.

Rehearsal – a practice run of the scene is usually done so the director can see how it will look before actual filming.

Resume – just like a work resume, this is your acting work resume. Check online for formatting help.

Rush Call – an opportunity to work on set once people are signed in. The reason for the rush call may be no-shows on set or that the director decided he needed more extras. Casting will usually call or email you directly to see if you are available right away to go to work.

Rolling – the film is rolling (recording), which means money in a production.

Screen Actors Guild (SAG) – a union (guild) of actors who are always in the midst of negotiations for their contract on their next film.

Set – the place where the filming is taking place. There may be many sets throughout the day.

Shooting – the scene is being marked to be used as footage.

Stand-In/Second Team – a stand-in for film and television is a person who substitutes for the actor *before* filming, for technical purposes such as lighting and rehearsals.

Taft-Hartley Act – a United States federal law greatly restricting the activities and power of labor unions. The Act, still effective, was sponsored by Senator Robert Taft and Representative Fred A. Hartley, Jr. The Taft-Hartley Act, amended the National Labor Relations Act (NLRA; informally the Wagner Act), which Congress passed in 1935. It has a special meaning in the entertainment industry. Specifically, for film and television actors, an actor not in the union who becomes a "principal performer" (says a line) is immediately eligible to join the Screen Actors Guild and is covered under the

SAG contract with the production company for 30 days, at which point he or she must either join SAG or cease working on any union productions. Once joining the union, the actor may not work on any non-union production, per the terms of the bylaws. This allows SAG to get around the rules forbidding closed shops by providing a mechanism for new members to join the union. (source: http://www.actor-preneur.com)

Transportation to Holding – once you park, usually at this location a van or bus will come by and pick up all extras and take them to set. Be prepared with your wardrobe and stuff to take with you.

Union (Guild) – an organized group of workers who come together to make decisions about the conditions of their work. Through union membership (SAG, AFTRA, etc.), workers can impact wages, work hours, benefits, workplace health and safety, and other work-related issues. Having support from the union to ensure fair treatment in the workplace is one of the key reasons people join. *Union Laws: see SAG rules for your state.*

Upgraded – means that if you are an extra on the set and are asked by the director to say a line you are now considered upgraded. You will need to mark your voucher with your upgraded information and have the PA sign off on it. You will also receive an increase in pay.

Wardrobe – the person(s) responsible to make sure that your clothes match the scene for that day. If the scene takes place in 1960 and you show up in FUBU™ jeans and a tank top, that will not work! Wardrobe may assign you something to wear that will need to be returned by the day's end.

Working Extra Kit – Jamie's generic term describing some things to take in a bag to set to stay occupied and not hungry, just in case.

Wrap – it's over. The end. Finito.

Voucher – your payment form that needs to be filled out at the beginning of each set. Take time in holding to do so. If you need to borrow any clothes from wardrobe they will keep your voucher. At the end of the day when you return your wardrobe you will get your voucher back. Then you can sign out for the day. Keep a copy for your records so you have proof of work for your pay.

NOTES: _____

_____

_____

_____

_____

_____

_____

_____

_____

_____

_____

_____

_____

_____

_____

_____

_____

_____

_____

_____

_____

_____

_____

_____

_____

_____

_____

NOTES: _____

_____

_____

_____

_____

_____

_____

_____

_____

_____

_____

_____

_____

_____

_____

_____

_____

_____

_____

_____

_____

_____

_____

_____

_____

_____

_____

_____

_____

NOTES: _____

_____

_____

_____

_____

_____

_____

_____

_____

_____

_____

_____

_____

_____

_____

_____

_____

_____

_____

_____

_____

_____

_____

_____

_____

_____

_____

_____

NOTES: _____

_____

_____

_____

_____

_____

_____

_____

_____

_____

_____

_____

_____

_____

_____

_____

_____

_____

_____

_____

_____

_____

_____

_____

_____

_____

_____

_____

_____

_____

_____

NOTES: _____

_____

_____

_____

_____

_____

_____

_____

_____

_____

_____

_____

_____

_____

_____

_____

_____

_____

_____

_____

_____

_____

_____

_____

_____

_____

_____

NOTES: _____

_____

_____

_____

_____

_____

_____

_____

_____

_____

_____

_____

_____

_____

_____

_____

_____

_____

_____

_____

_____

_____

_____

_____

_____

_____

_____

_____